The Stripple Stones, a 'circle-henge' on Bodmin Moor

Ancient Cornwall

Paul White

D0300833

Tor Mark Press • Redruth

The Tor Mark series

This reprint 2004

First published 2000 by Tor Mark Press, PO Box 4, Redruth, Cornwall, TR16 5YX

ISBN 0-85025-382-9

© 2000 Tor Mark Press

The photograph on page 28 was taken by kind permission of English Heritage
The map on page 32 is by Graham Hallowell

Printed in Great Britain by R Booth Ltd, Mabe, Cornwall

Introduction

Part of Cornwall's allure is that much of its past is there to see in solid and enduring granite. This book is an introduction to the visible remains of the county's prehistory, from around 4000 BC to the departure of the Romans around AD 400.

The earliest human constructions in Cornwall date back some 6000 years, from very near the earliest days when people began living in settled communities rather than roving as hunter-gatherers, or following herds of wild animals in seasonal migrations.

For lasting monuments the ancient people chose to build in stone, although their houses were probably built of wood. In time the land became deforested, so that stone was used for houses too. And the stones have lasted. Whereas in much of England prehistory is the preserve of the archaeologist, in Cornwall academic knowledge is not vital – anyone can appreciate the massive 'quoits', the stone circles, the ancient field walls and the remains of huts, so numerous in some areas that it is hard to miss them – though it may help to have a little background knowledge.

The key areas for the visitor are those with granite outcrops, particularly West Penwith (the peninsula west of Penzance and St Ives) and Bodmin Moor. There are also many other sites spread around the county. Please see the map on page 32.

Archaeological periods

Archaeologists need labels to apply to the different periods of pre-history, for ease of discussion. The main periods covered in this book are:

The **Neolithic** or New Stone Age, which followed the Old and Middle Stone Ages. This is when people first began to grow crops and maintain animal herds near a fixed settlement. In Cornwall the Neolithic is roughly 4500 BC–2200 BC.

The **Bronze Age**, roughly 2200 BC–700 BC. During this period the technology of metal-working in bronze was known, but most people continued to use stone tools: bronze was so expensive that it was largely confined to prestige objects for the powerful.

The **Iron Age** started around 700 BC. Iron smelting was relatively easy (once it had been discovered!) and metal use became quite common for everyday tools. Conventionally this period is said to have ended with the arrival of the Romans in AD 43, but in Cornwall that event seems hardly to have changed the way of life. Here the Iron Age can be regarded as continuing until Britain ceased to be part of the Roman Empire around AD 400.

It should be stressed that these periods shade into one another: there were in real life no sudden technological changes. In the recent past archaeologists assumed that each change, even in pottery styles, came about as the result of an invasion of new people: today's archaeologists prefer to stress the continuities, with new inventions in technology and religion being adopted by the existing people rather than brought by waves of invaders. Trade contacts between peoples widely separated are known to have been common: a few people were well-travelled and carried new ideas with them, although most never went far from their homes.

The easiest way to travel was by sea. Look at a map and you may judge Cornwall 'remote' because today we think in terms of land transport: look at the map with a sea-goer's eye and you will understand why prehistoric Cornwall was right at the heart of the lively communities on the Atlantic seaboard.

The 'centre-stone' of Boscawen-ûn circle (actually the stone is off-centre and the 'circle' is an ellipse) may have been originally upright, or perhaps it was always at an angle. It is still used as a kind of altar by modern pagans

Trethevy Quoit, at the south-east corner of Bodmin Moor, is particularly well preserved. The capstone may have been designed to be slightly tilted, though the present angle is due to dilapidation

Penwith chamber tombs, or 'quoits'

These distinctive structures are found mainly in Penwith, although perhaps the finest example is Trethevy Quoit on the edge of Bodmin Moor. Their exact age is unknown, but before 3000 BC is probable, and as early as 4000 BC quite possible.

Some, including Zennor Quoit (SW 469380) and Trethevy Quoit (SX 259688), have a totally enclosed chamber with a miniature porch in front of it, and are known as 'portal dolmens'. Others just have a chamber, as at Chûn Quoit (SW 402339). In all cases they were probably originally covered by a mound or cairn, the edge of which was marked by a kerb of stones (still partly visible at Chûn) but it is possible that for the portal dolmens the architecturally handsome façade was visible through a gap in the mound. The porch area may have been used for ceremonies.

Such massive structures would have taken much effort to build and were clearly important to their communities. The great sloping capstones weigh around 20 tonnes.

Above: Zennor Quoit, showing the 'portal' or porch within which ceremonies were probably conducted

Below: Chûn Quoit

The exact purpose of the quoits is unknown. They contained communal burials – possibly of individual bones retrieved from decomposed bodies rather than fresh burials – but they may have been a focal point for the community; perhaps they were like our parish churches, which contain burials in and around them but are certainly not thought of as mausoleums.

Later people re-used these great structures for their own ceremonies and burials, and of course they attracted early tomb robbers, so little remains intact for archaeologists.

Lanyon Quoit (shown below) is one of Cornwall's most popular antiquities, being beside the road at SW 430337. It is very atmospheric but unfortunately not totally authentic.

The structure collapsed in a storm in 1815, and funds were raised by public subscription for a rebuilding in 1824, but some of the supporting stones had broken in the fall. Before this disaster, it was apparently possible to ride a horse under the capstone. The shape of the covering mound is not at all clear: there may have been a long barrow, or there may have been two smaller circular mounds.

Ballowal Barrow, also known as Carn Gloose, a massive entrance grave near St Just-in-Penwith

Entrance graves

These are very common on Scilly, where some fifty survive, and they are also found in Brittany. A dozen have been identified in Penwith. They consisted of a mound of earth or stones piled over a stone structure, with a low corridor covered by multiple cap-stones leading to a central underground chamber.

The Tregiffian chamber tomb

The most dramatic example is Ballowal Barrow, also known as Carn Gloose, near St Just (SW 355312), which probably began as a Neolithic 'quoit' and was then adapted in the Bronze Age with a great conical central cairn (rising above the level of what remains) surrounded by a wide flat collar.

More typical is the Tregiffian chamber tomb (SW 430244), on the roadside very near the Merry Maidens stone circle. This was probably 12 metres in diameter, and has been partly destroyed by the road. It may date to 2500 BC, but contained a later burial which was radio-carbon dated to 1900 BC.

Stowe's Pound

Just behind the famous Cheesewring and within easy walking distance of the Hurlers stone circles and Rillaton Barrow, Stowe's Pound (SX 259725) is a massively constructed hilltop fortification consisting of two enclosures, believed to be of late Neolithic or early Bronze Age date – though nobody really knows!

The ramparts are made from stones, now collapsed, and would have been some five or six metres high, hundreds of metres in length. Such massive walls must have been built for warfare rather than as a defence against animals. There are remains of round huts within the outer enclosure and on the surrounding hills, but these may be later than the enclosure itself.

Most Neolithic houses were probably wooden (built before the upland woods were all felled and timber came into short supply) and rectangular in shape. The typical Bronze Age upland hut consisted of a circular stone wall, interrupted by a doorway with jambs, and roofed over with a conical wood and thatch structure. However, it must be stressed that opportunities for dating stone structures are quite rare even when they are excavated, since the acid soils of the moors have destroyed most of the organic finds needed for radio-carbon dating.

It is known that there were also extensive lowland settlements, but their wooden structures have left no trace at all.

The rampart of the outer enclosure of Stowe's Pound

King Arthur's Hall

This mysterious structure on Bodmin Moor (SX 130776) should on no account be missed. Nobody knows what it is or when it was built – though it certainly has nothing to do with King Arthur! Personally I suspect it is Neolithic and is a kind of rectangular 'henge'. Henges preceded stone circles and normally consist of a circular ditch and bank, sometimes with a stone circle inside.

The best henge in the south-west is in fact within an hour's walk of King Arthur's Hall – the Stripple Stones at SX 143752. (You can get there by footpath and Access Land if you walk east to Garrow Bronze Age settlement, then turn south, crossing the streams by two bridges at SX 145775: the henge itself is a little unexciting but it's a gloriously scenic and lonely walk.)

King Arthur's Hall consists of a substantial bank on the inside of which are vertical flat stones (looking like chair backs for Arthur's knights before they got their round table!) surrounding a marshy rectangle in the middle. It is the size and shape of a small municipal swimming pool. It may well be one of the most significant sites in Cornwall, yet the uncertainty of the archaeologists over its age and function means it is often ignored.

Bronze age graves

Whereas Neolithic graves were communal, from about 2500 BC people seem to have been buried in separate graves. The graves which survive are those which involved most effort – the 'state funerals' of powerful or culturally significant individuals.

Typically they were buried in a 'cist' like the one in the photograph, a simple granite box with a lid. (After about 2000 BC, the cremated remains rather than the body were placed within a cist.) This cist was then covered with a round barrow of earth, or a cairn of stones. Many such round barrows are still to be seen, often grouped on a skyline. (There are striking clusters beside the A30, at SW 761482 and SW 845538.) Because they sometimes contained valuable grave goods, such barrows were almost all robbed in medieval or more recent times, leaving nothing for modern archaeologists except the cist.

There were many designs of barrow – bowl and bell, ring cairns, and so on, and they were often constructed in stages over many years. The ravages of time make them all look rather similar to the casual visitor; the best is Rillaton Barrow (SX 260719).

In the example below, the barrow has largely eroded, though an outer circular bank remains, and within that a ring of stones.

Stone circles

At least 25 circles survive in Cornwall, though where the stones are small or have fallen the circle may be difficult to find, especially in summer when undergrowth envelops them. The circles illustrated are all well-preserved and relatively easy of access.

The experience of visiting one of these circles is quite different from visiting Stonehenge. They are on a very much smaller scale. Here you are often alone with the stones – no turnstiles, no tunnels, and above all no crowds. It is hard not to be aware that these places were once sacred, and indeed they are still places of pilgrimage and worship for some people, because offerings of flowers or beads are frequently placed at these sites.

The Boscawen-ûn circle (ûn is pronounced 'oon'; park at SW 410277 whence the footpath is obvious, but may not be a legal right of way) is mentioned in a medieval Welsh manuscript as one of the three main Gorsedds (cultural meeting places) of the Britons, and the modern Cornish Gorsedd first met here in 1928 – but the circle's origin is of course much older. Cornwall's stone circles are all thought to date from between 2500 and 1600 BC.

Another circle worth visiting in the same general area of Penwith is called the Merry Maidens (SW 433245), though I find it lacks some of the atmosphere of other circles, being planted in what is now a well-grazed field. In its immediate vicinity and clearly associated with it are various standing stones (called 'menhirs') including the Pipers (see page 20) as well as the much older Tregiffian entrance grave (see page 10). It is very common for monuments of different kinds to be grouped together, though the significance of the groupings is not understood.

It is also quite common for two or three circles to be almost touching one another, as at the Hurlers on Bodmin Moor (SX 258714), where there were three, of which two are still clearly visible. Near King Arthur's Hall one circle is marked on the map (SX 135775), but half of a second circle is visible right next to it, and a third is just out of sight due to stone walls, at SX 137773.

Above: Boscawen-ûn circle, celebrated in the Middle Ages as one of the three main Gorsedds of Britain
Below: the Merry Maidens, between Penzance and St Buryan

Above: Fernacre stone circle with Rough Tor in the background
Below: The Hurlers – three circles closely aligned

Stannon stone circle on Bodmin Moor. This forms part of a 'ritual complex' of circles together with Fernacre and Louden Hill

A triangle of circles is to be found just to the north of King Arthur's Hall, at Stannon (SX 125800), Fernacre (SX 145799) and the Louden Hill Circle (fragmentary, at SX 132795). The first two are very atmospheric, and Fernacre is well worth the walk: if you start from the Rough Tor car park (SX 138819) you will pass through two Bronze Age villages on the way.

Such combinations of monuments give rise to the idea of 'ley lines', which are supposedly lines of power within the earth. Unfortunately ley lines seem susceptible only to the somewhat subjective art of dowsing. There is no scientific evidence that ley lines exist, and every reason to suppose they are wishful thinking.

The Trippet Stones

Much the same might be said of the theory that the monuments were astronomical observatories. This cannot be ruled out, but many of the stones have moved naturally from their original position, due to soil creep, or been replaced by enthusiastic Victorian antiquarians, so they may not be exactly where the builders intended. And since there are rather a lot of heavenly bodies, and a lot of dates in the year, some alignments should be expected by chance alone.

There do however seem to be crude alignments of sunrise or sunset over neighbouring hills, at least from some of the Bodmin Moor circles. The jury is still out on anything more sophisticated.

The Trippet Stones (SX 131750) are another attractive Bodmin Moor circle, a short distance from a minor road, and exhibit two features typical of many circles. Many of the stones are missing, having found a new life as gateposts, door-jambs or lintels; and those that remain are surrounded by little pools, caused by erosion when cattle use the stones as rubbing posts. (In Penwith, where every other little field seems to contain a standing stone, a significant proportion of them are rubbing posts erected relatively recently for the animals!)

Duloe stone circle. Its stones are massive and full of individual character

One circle quite unlike anything else in Cornwall is that at Duloe (SX236583) between Looe and Liskeard. Most surviving prehistoric features occur on high ground, either because that is where our ancestors chose to live or more probably because features on lower ground have been destroyed by subsequent land use. It is also possible that monuments on lower ground continued to be built in wood, especially if the circles were symbolic of groves, and the standing long-stones symbolic of trees.

The circle at Duloe is in a field behind houses, to the east of the road through the village. It is very small in circumference – only about 11 metres – but the stones are massive, and instead of being granite they are white quartz. When newly built, it must have been astonishingly bright. It is estimated that it would have taken nearly forty people to lift some of the stones.

Menhirs or long-stones

These standing stones are mainly concentrated in West Penwith, possibly because it had become treeless by the time they were erected. In other areas wooden posts may have continued in use: perhaps they were like the totem poles of the native Americans.

Those shown here, the Pipers (SW 435248), are just out of sight from the Merry Maidens circle, and presumably part of the same ritual complex.

The tradition of erecting single stones never ceased in the upland areas of south-west Britain; in the post-Roman period inscribed stones were used as memorials and then in the Middle Ages great numbers of beautifully carved crosses were set up – some of which may well have been recycled Bronze Age menhirs. Even today, upright stones will be found beside tracks, carrying the farm name, or marking the entrance to an industrial estate. It is a living tradition.

The Pipers

The Mên-an-tol

The name simply means 'stone-with-a-hole-in-it'. This famously enigmatic monument lies (SW 426350) in the middle of a prehistoric landscape, but the surrounding monuments cover a period of 3000 years or more, so dating the Mên-an-tol is a matter of guesswork. Most people guess Bronze Age. Nor is it known what its function was, or whether it was once part of some larger monument. There are other holed stones in Cornwall, and also on Dartmoor, and folklore claimed they could cure disease.

Robert Hunt wrote 'If scrofulous children are passed naked through the Mên-an-tol three times, and then drawn on the grass three times against the sun, it is felt by the faithful that much has been done towards insuring a speedy cure. Even men and women who have been afflicted with spinal diseases, or who have suffered from scrofulous taint, have been drawn through this magic stone, which all declare still retains its ancient virtues.

'If two brass pins are carefully laid across each other on the top edge of this stone, any question put to the rock will be answered by the pins acquiring, through some unknown agency, a peculiar motion.'

Hut circles

Across the higher moors of West Penwith, particularly between St Just and St Ives, and in the central parts of Bodmin Moor, lie isolated homes and often whole villages which have remained almost undisturbed since they were deserted 3000 years ago. They are marked on the OS maps as 'hut circles' or 'settlement'.

The huts vary in size, and some were just outhouses, but they average six metres in diameter, with a clearly marked doorway, sometimes paved, and occasionally an identifiable hearth or bed-space. The low stone wall supported a conical roof; like all the other wooden parts of the structure this has long since rotted away, but many of the houses were quite spacious: Cornish rural housing standards of the eighteenth century BC were not significantly worse than those of the eighteenth century AD.

Standing or sitting in these ancient homes it is easy to imagine for ourselves the daily lives of their owners: indeed one almost feels like an intruder, literally within the domestic circle.

Probably the most interesting place from which to explore is the Rough Tor car park (SX 138819). From here you can head for the Bronze Age village centred on 140815, a further village with a well defined system of little fields at 144803 and the Fernacre stone circle. A medieval long-house, Louden Farm, is also worth exploring at 138803. You will find the remains look very like the Bronze Age hut circles, except that they are rectangular.

The presence together of Bronze Age and medieval remains is no coincidence. It is all a matter of climate change.

The whole idea of farming – stock rearing first and then arable – was a major technological leap. This is what marks the beginning of the Neolithic period. Hunting, fishing and gathering did not cease but became less important. In Cornwall this first occurred around 4500 BC. The British climate had been improving since the end of the last Ice Age. Around 3800 BC an upsurge in El Niño activity sparked a dramatic increase in average world temperatures – a rise of as much as 2°C perhaps within a decade.

Bronze Age settlement to the south of Rough Tor

The uplands then may have been preferable to the lowlands for settlement. The weather was warmer and much drier than it is now. The lightly wooded uplands were easier to clear than the densely wooded and often badly drained lowlands. Growing crops on the hills was quite easy. Only later, as a result of overuse, did the soils become peaty and infertile. Around 1000 BC, as a result of worsening climate, it proved easier to farm the lowlands, and the settlements we can explore today were deserted, though their lands would have been used for summer grazing.

After 2000 years or so another improvement of the climate, and shortage of land through increased population, led to medieval resettlement. That stopped abruptly with the Black Death in 1349 – not because upland farming families were disproportionately stricken but because the climate had, from about 1300, worsened again. The survivors were able to find better livelihoods in the lowlands. In later periods there have been isolated farms rearing stock, but no arable farming, and many areas have never been reclaimed except as common grazing.

Left: At first sight this looks like a Bronze Age ruin, but it is actually the remains of a rectangular long-house at Louden Farm

Right: This ancient reave seems to mark the boundary between two neighbouring villages on the western side of Rough Tor, with an equally ancient track bisecting it

The Bronze Age people had sophisticated and extensive land divisions, now called 'reaves'. These were low walls, probably surmounted by a live hedge, or in a more flexible arrangement by a wattle fence or uprooted thorn bushes, to control livestock.

Some village field systems, for example Garrow on Bodmin Moor (SX 146778) were neatly divided into 'strips', not unlike the medieval 'stitches' which survive at Forrabury near Boscastle.

Iron Age hill forts

In the Bronze Age, certainly from 2000-700BC, people seem to have lived peaceably in sprawling undefended villages, but after that period there was apparently an increasing need for self-defence. Iron Age farmsteads were often 'rounds' – surrounded by a small earthwork – and there were increasing numbers of hill-forts and promontory forts. Many of these were used until the Roman period and some were refurbished in the post-Roman period, another time of unrest and uncertainty.

A particularly attractive hill-fort is Castle Dore (SX 103548) near Fowey, which is incomparable in May when the slopes are covered with spring flowers. This is also the legendary home of King Mark of Cornwall, who may have lived in the sixth or early seventh century AD, and of his nephew (or perhaps son) Tristan. Unfortunately for the legend, it is far from certain that the fort was reused at this time

Whereas most of the forts are earthworks, and often the earth banks and ditches have eroded so that they are less than impressive, Chûn Castle (SW 405339) is built of massive rocks and is 85 metres in diameter, with two walls the inner of which stood six metres high; it is still more than head height and nearly five metres thick.

Within the walls is a well, lined with stone, and a tin-smelting furnace was found here. Presumably the inhabitants controlled the local tin trade. We know the fort was occupied around 300-200 BC and that it was reoccupied during the post-Roman period.

Chûn Castle was occupied around 300-200 BC and its owners probably controlled the supply of Cornish tin to the Mediterranean traders who visited these shores

The well at Chûn Castle. Huts from the sixth century AD show that the site was re-occupied in those dangerous times

Trevelgue Head, near Newquay, in a sea mist. The huge defensive earthworks improved a naturally secure site

Promontory forts

There are over thirty known promontory forts in Cornwall, all fun to visit because of the cliff scenery, but at some of them the archaeological remains are little more than eroded earthworks at the neck. The most interesting are Trevelgue Head at Newquay (SW 825630), Treryn Dinas near St Buryan (SW 396223) and the Rumps near Polzeath (SW 934811).

One theory is that some or even all these forts were built by the Veneti, the people who lived in southern Brittany and are known to have traded with Cornwall. They might have used them in the way that seventeenth century Europeans established trading forts on the African coast. The Veneti were only subdued by Julius Caesar with great difficulty. He had to build a fleet to overcome their habit of shutting themselves in their Breton promontory forts, waiting for the Romans to besiege them and then, when the Romans broke in, embarking in one of their massive ships to fight another day. There is every reason to think that the Cornish learned from them, but no real reason to believe that the Veneti actually constructed the Cornish forts.

The 'fogou' at Carn Euny

Courtyard houses

In the Iron Age most people continued to live in round huts, as had their predecessors, but an interesting variant appeared in West Penwith about 500 BC and lasted until the end of the Roman period. These houses have a central open courtyard around which are individual rooms – living accommodation, workrooms, store rooms and cattle pens.

Two such sites are easily accessible to the public, Chysauster (SW 473350: English Heritage) and Carn Euny (SW 402288: Cornwall Heritage Trust). Both are fascinating but my own favourite is Carn Euny, not just because it is (at the time of writing) free, but because in addition to the houses you can explore a magnificent 'fogou'. Fogous are underground passages, sometimes as at Carn Euny leading to a sizeable underground room.

The purpose of fogous remains uncertain: cold storage is the most likely, but as a hiding place or for some ritual use are both entirely possible.

The Romans

There is very little evidence of Roman control in Cornwall. It is probable that when the Romans invaded in AD 43 the rulers of Cornwall welcomed them and were then left to run their own affairs as before. One Roman fort at Nanstallon near Bodmin was briefly occupied, and there are five third century stones, the best example to see being inside Tintagel parish church.

They are often referred to as milestones, but perhaps functioned more like advertising hoardings – 'Your Imperial Government – investing in roads'. Or they may have been datum points for measuring distances on a British trackway. There is no evidence that any road in Cornwall was constructed to Roman standards.

One interesting site is Lelant churchyard (SW 548377). This is almost square in shape and some believe it to have been a small Roman fort, sited to overlook the Hayle estuary which was on a major trading route. After the Romans left, Christian missionaries from an Irish colony in south Wales (or were they invaders intent on further colonising?) were to land here and be martyred by the local king Teudrig who had his stronghold at Lelant – perhaps occupying the former Roman fort. But this is guesswork.

Lelant churchyard – possibly in origin a small Roman fort

The Mên scryfa

The Mên scryfa

This 'written-on stone' from the sixth century (SW 427353, near the Mên-an-tol) is one of many such monuments from the post-Roman period recording an individual – in this case Rialobran, son of Cunoval. The names mean 'Royal Raven' and 'Famous chieftain' – only the powerful received such memorials.

Before the Romans brought Latin, there was no written language, so it is likely that the earlier uninscribed menhirs were also memorials to famous individuals.

Of the post-Roman stones, some are in Latin, some in Irish ogham script, and some in both. Some are definitely Christian, with a cross or a chi-rho symbol, but others including the Mên scryfa may well be pre-Christian. The date of Christianisation of Cornwall, and its manner, is currently a matter of learned debate and the stones are an important part of the evidence – but with written sources such as the Mên scryfa, we have now passed the dividing line from 'prehistoric' into 'historic' times.

The Rocky Valley carvings

This site (SX073893) is included as an example of how difficult it is to date a piece of stone. On a cliff wall inside Rocky Valley, a noted beauty spot between Tintagel and Boscastle, are two maze carvings. The design is as old as the Bronze Age. These were first reported only in the mid twentieth century and 'authenticated' by the late Dr Ralegh Radford. It is odd that no earlier antiquarian mentions them.

They lie immediately behind a ruined mill and there is a distinct possibility that they were carved by the miller one day when there was no other work to do! The designs on mill stones had to be re-engraved at frequent intervals, as they quickly became blunted, so millers certainly had the skills needed.

This uncertainty has not prevented the site from becoming a New Age shrine and the riddle of the mazes makes a fine excuse – if you need one – for a walk along the cliffs from Tintagel, passing on the way the Iron Age promontory fort of Willapark.

One of the Rocky Valley carvings – ancient or modern?

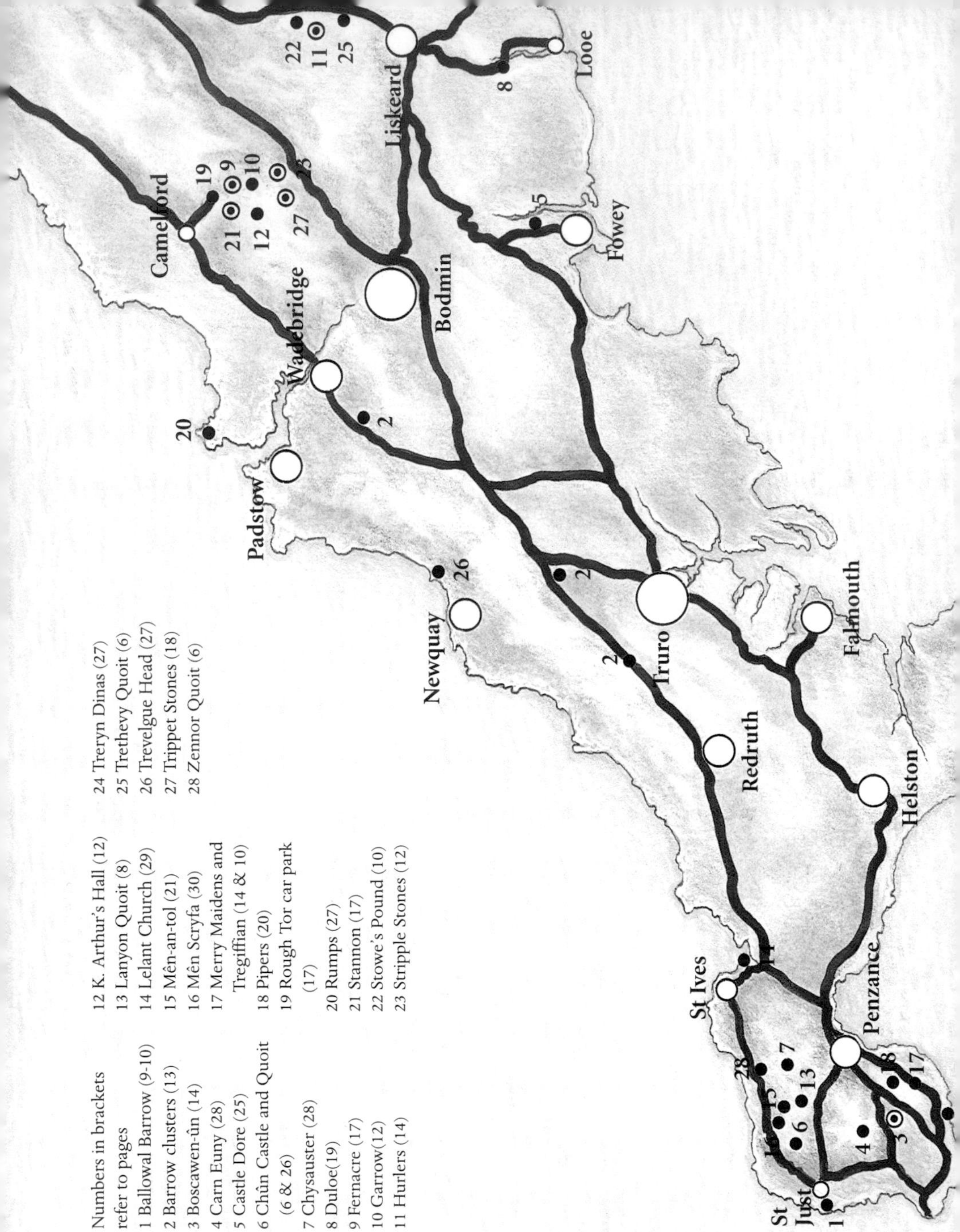
Numbers in brackets refer to pages
1 Ballowal Barrow (9-10)
2 Barrow clusters (13)
3 Boscawen-ûn (14)
4 Carn Euny (28)
5 Castle Dore (25)
6 Chûn Castle and Quoit (6 & 26)
7 Chysauster (28)
8 Duloe(19)
9 Fernacre (17)
10 Garrow(12)
11 Hurlers (14)
12 K. Arthur's Hall (12)
13 Lanyon Quoit (8)
14 Lelant Church (29)
15 Mên-an-tol (21)
16 Mên Scryfa (30)
17 Merry Maidens and Tregiffian (14 & 10)
18 Pipers (20)
19 Rough Tor car park (17)
20 Rumps (27)
21 Stannon (17)
22 Stowe's Pound (10)
23 Stripple Stones (12)
24 Treryn Dinas (27)
25 Trethevy Quoit (6)
26 Trevelgue Head (27)
27 Trippet Stones (18)
28 Zennor Quoit (6)
Camelford
Liskeard
Looe
Fowey
Bodmin
Wadebridge
Padstow
Newquay
Truro
Falmouth
Redruth
Helston
St Ives
Penzance
St Just

Readers wanting to study Cornwall's prehistory a little further are recommended to read *Cornovia* by Craig Weatherhill.